IT'S *All* GOD

Carolyn Cole

Copyright © 2015 by Carolyn Cole

It's All God
by Carolyn Cole

Printed in the United States of America.

ISBN 9781498484626

All rights reserved solely by the author. The author guarantees all contents are original and do not infringe upon the legal rights of any other person or work. No part of this book may be reproduced in any form without the permission of the author. The views expressed in this book are not necessarily those of the publisher.

Unless otherwise indicated, Scripture quotations taken from Scripture quotations taken from the Holy Bible, New International Version (NIV). Copyright © 1973, 1978, 1984, 2011 by Biblica, Inc.™. Used by permission. All rights reserved.

www.xulonpress.com

ACKNOWLEDGEMENT

I would like to thank the one, that without His presence in my life, I would not have been able to complete this task. For without Him, I am nothing and yet He makes me everything I am. Lord I know that my very being is dependent on you, and I will accept all of your requirements just to be called your child. I stretch my arms wide and bow my head low and ask "Lord am I worthy" ?

I would also like to thank Pastor Bernard and First Lady Linda Curry for allowing me to present my poems to my church family...Mt. Zion United Church Of God, where the word is always taught in truth and understanding. There are some very special friends in my life, who has always given me support, love and advice. I want to take this time to say thanks to all of you for your personal help and opinions. Minister Gladys Lawrence, Sisters Diane, Judy, Daphne and Barbara D. Also a very special thanks to Elder Saundra Swinton and Sandra Williams for always lending an ear to listen. As an only child, I always knew there was something other than siblings missing in my life. Not that I'm complaining, because being an only child does have it's perks. But it was the lack of knowing God as I know Him now. He has given me more sisters and brothers than I ever could have imagined. My Mt. Zion church family. For this I say..."Thank you Father God."

TABLE OF CONTENTS

1. THE BLESSING PARTY 9
2. HE'S COMING BACK 10
3. ALL IN A DAY 11
4. A CORNERED SOUL 12
5. ASSUMPTION 13
6. CROWN OF THORNS 14
7. JESUS IS MINDING THE DOOR 15
8. A TEARDROP FROM FAITH 16
9. MY RESTFUL SPIRIT 17
10. MY ROBE OF DEEDS 18
11. TAKE ME TO A PLACE 19
12. LIVING IN DARKNESS 20
13. FORGIVENESS 21
14. LET IT GO...LET IT BE 22
15. THE STORM 23
16. LOVE 24
17. THE EARNED INSCRIPTION 25
18. IN A VISION 26
19. A SILENT WHISPER 27
20. CHANGE THOSE CLOTHES 28
21. BLOOD SHED 29
22. HELP ME LORD 30
23. COVER THESE BONES 31
24. A WORD FROM YOU 32
25. HEAVEN BOUND 33
26. MY INHERITANCE 34
27. OH PRECIOUSLY SILENT ROBE 35
28. THE BAPTISM 36
29. THOU PREPAREST A TABLE 37
30. UNDER HIS CLOAK 38
31. UNCHAINED SEED OF FAITH 39
32. COVERED SMILE 40
33. FROM YOUR FATHER 41

34. HELP. 42
35. HOW DO I SAY THANKS 43
36. LAST NIGHTS BREEZE. 44
37. THAT SONG. 45
38. MY SOUL BELONGS TO YOU 46
39. UNDER HIS WING 47
40. IMAGINE 48
41. JESUS OF NAZARETH. 49

THE BLESSING PARTY

Come on down..........
                The table is set and covered with a white linen tablecloth
                Our bowls are made of sparkling crystal, our utensils of pure gold

Have a seat
                Enjoy a bowl of life: Your waiters will be the Angels, coming by the way of Glory
                      Your head waiter is — —-Mercy !
                      Your head chef is — — —-Grace !
We are serving — — — — — — — —A big pot of life and a side order of faith
For dessert— — — — — — — — — —"Sweet Po-Blessing Pie"
Take a sniff — —Smell that aroma of this tantalizing soup
                There's no other soup like it
We took all of your problems, added a little Isaiah 41:10, let it broil in our hearts and minds.

We took your desires, seperated "em" from the flesh, marinated "em", added "em" to the pot and let "em" simmer. Next we took a cup of hope and coated it with care, prayer and praise, along with a big pinch of determination- (for that added flavor)—Sprinkled lots of Love and let it simmer to perfectiion.
                For You Are Now At The Blessing Party
Have a cup of salvation..... Sip it while it's hot
                WARNING — —DO NOT BLOW TO COOL !!!!!!!
                For you are apt to blow away your blessing
                YOUR BLESSINGS ARE IN THE STEAM
Step on over to the dessert table and have a slice of "Sweet Po-Blessing Pie"
                It's made to bless you in all your everyday needs
           Enjoy everything that is yours— —ENJOY LIFE, ENJOY LOVE,
                    ENJOY YOUR "SWEET PO-BLESSING PIE" UMM UMMM

HE'S COMING BACK

On one day, when we least expect it
Our Jesus is coming back
He'll be delivered, from the wounds and sins
That were placed on him, when He left.
We'll look at His hands, His feet and His side
To be sure that it is He
But He'll be healed, from that beating He took
On that day He set us free.
He'll be sanctified, by our Father's hands
Touched by His Holy truth
He'll be glorified and exemplified
From the peoples pain and abuse.
He'll stretch out his arms, and open his hands
With the judgement book inside
He'll call our names one by one
To explain how we've lived our lives.
There'll be prophesying, by His chosen ones
From the Holy Spirit as foretold
There'll be knees bending, and voices accending
From the bottom of our very souls.
And when you are called, to speak your peace
No thought are you to have
On what you'll say, on that day
For the Holy Spirit will reign.
Oh what a day that will be
When we stand before the throne
And that league of angels, will take our hands
To safely guide us home.

ALL IN A DAY

They had an unusual trial one day
Where Jesus was being charged
And found Him guilty of unjust crimes
Which Pilate played no part
Some slapped His face, some whipped His back
While others whispered and laughed
Looking at Him being unjustly punished
For things done back in the past
They walked our Jesus up a hill
To a place called calvary
And there they placed Him on a cross
And nailed his hands and feet
And as they raised that cross up high
For all the world to see
He was looking down on them
The same as He does today
The angels started praying
While watching his mother Mary
Her tears were soltly flowing
As time seem to tarry
And the blood from Him ran freelly
For He was torn and left with scars
No understanding did they have
That He was the son of God
He paid the price upon that cross
Where all our sins remain
And on the cross was left the blood
Of this our blessed lamb.
That Holy blood, that redeeming blood,
That powerful blood of Jesus.
Oh how it flowed, to save our souls
As He so lovingly freed us.

A CORNERED SOUL

I saw a man, old and frail
Sitting in the corner alone
Staring at his hands, while in a daze
As if time had taken a hold
He placed his face, in the palm of his hands
Mind set on that sacred place,
Where Jesus abides, and hopes alive
As a smile came over his face
The wrinkles and folds, have taken their form
Making crevices of his skin
And a whisper of air, gently blew
With a soft and fragrant wind
For he's one of the last , of his kind
And he knows that his time is near
But he's not ready to leave this place,
He has something he wants us to hear
He talks about a man called Jesus
Who walked this earth before
Giving sight to the blind, and healing the lame
And a spirit like none other to come
He talks about a king, that lives on high
Whose crown is beyond compare
And a beautiful place called Heaven
And how he's going there
So as I watched and listened
To that man that caught my eye
I knew he'd been talking with Jesus
By the shadowed light that shined
For the glory of God encamped him
This wise and feeble man
That was sitting there in the corner
With his face in the palm of his hands.

ASSUMPTION

And when they took you from the cross, they placed you in a tomb,
and rolled a stone to keep you in, or so they had assumed..

They led Jesus to the cross that day
And thought they'd won for a fact.
They thought they'd rid themselves of Him
They thought he'd never come back.
But He took all our sins away
That day on Calvary,
And carried them a whole lot further
Further than we could see.
He took them to a place of darkness
And there He decided to stay,
Fighting with the lost ones there
To show that He is the way.
Satan, corruption, and the grave
Gave it all they had,
But they could not hold Him there
Not even at the bottom of hell.
For they had lived in this place
And never seen the light
So once again, they assumed
That they had won the fight.
He won that battle, and gained respect
And they assumed that He was through,
Then he arose, with all power in His hands
From that fight for me and you.

CROWN OF THORNS

Never did they know,
That crown of thorns He wore,
Would be a crown of peace
To put aside, our disbelief
And make the unknowing cease.

Never did they know,
That crown of thorns He wore,
Was packed with so much love
Touched by our Holy Father
Who sits so high above.

Never did they know,
That crown of thorns He wore,
Would make the angels cry and sing
Sing a song of woe.

Never did they know ,
The crown of thorns He wore,
Would one day set them free
That powerful crown, placed on His head
Placed there for you and me!!

JESUS IS MINDING THE DOOR

I was always told......
Walk straight, with your head held high,
I didn't understand the reasoning then,
And I often wondered why.
I was always told.....
Keep your eyes on heaven above,
For there is a gated room up there,
And Jesus is minding the door.
Sometimes you'll feel like you're all alone
But your body and soul are protected
Within the walls of a righteous room,
Where you'll feel the spirit steering,.
Now there is no need to worry,
About problems in this place,
Cause you are overly guarded,
Behind the door, behind the gate.
The spirit will lay you at His feet,
And your soul will feel afloat,
As you rest behind that door,
In the room that's filled with hope.
There you can praise Him deeply,
Contented all through the day,
And there you'll find all peace of mind,
While your soul is tucked away.
For your spirit will be lifted,
And you'll learn to walk up straight,
After your visit to the room,
That has the door, behind the gate.
For you are there because of love,
And protected to the core,
And there's no need to rush your time,
Cause Jesus is minding the door.

A TEARDROP FROM FAITH

I saw the face of a lady, lying face up toward the sky
She was so still and peaceful, as one teardrop filled her eye
She had an expression of contentment, as she lie so straight and still
With the look of anticipation, of hope in that one tear.....and then she spoke

This tear I shed is filled
With joy and praise galore
And all the happiness for your future
With the salvation you're hoping for
This tear is filled with compassion
For all the world to see
For I've had a glimps of His glory
And it's locked up in this one tear
And this tear is not just water
But the solution with answers to all
And it has traveled from heaven
For it once was a tear of God
This tear that I shed so humbly
Is not only shed for me
But for everyone who loves Jesus
And His face you want to see

For that tear was filled with holiness
That she could not contain
And the look in her eyes were telling me
That she'd seen the promise land
And as she turned her face away
That tear glistened in the air
Then dropped onto the pillow
And slowly disappeared

MY RESTFUL SPIRIT

As the spirit of the Lord rest over my soul,
I began to walk
I felt my burdens being lifted away
And a quiver in my talk
For I could not withhold the peace
That nestled within my heart
As the spirit of the Lord rest over my soul
I began to walk

My feet were like the angels' wings
Lifting me higher than high
And as I thought of your love so deep
I began to cry
This spirit so sweet, and oh so clean
Came upon me suddenly
It made me want to sing and shout
Leaving no room for worry or doubt
And now my soul is at ease
My God, my Father, please never leave

As the spirit of the Lord rest over my soul
I began to walk

The spirit of despair, tried to show it's face
I began to walk
There's no room for you, in this spiritual place
I began to walk
I cried, "Thank you Jesus",,,for loving me
I began to walk
Then more of His spirit I did see, I began to walk

When the spirit of the Lord rest over my soul
I began to walk
Thank you Jesus for my spiritual steps.

MY ROBE OF DEEDS

OH MY HEAVENLY FATHER!!

Let me use my righteous deeds,
As silken threads of gold,
To pull through, the eye of the needle,
Made up of the love you hold.
Let this mortal body,
Be fitted to a tee,
And let this robe of deeds I knit,
Be especially made for me.
Let me knit my robe for glory,
As the righteous saints would do,
To wear it up in heaven one day,
As only the angels could.
Let me look up and pray,
Stay busy and obey,
The precious words of you my Father,
And keep my priorities straight.
Let my mind stay on Jesus,
To keep my heart renewed,
For all the things I need to know,
That my righteous deeds should do.
Refresh me Lord, if you must,
To ensure that I am right,
To make this robe, that I knit,
Be perfect in your eyesight.
And when it's all fully complete,
And you call my name one day,
Let my glorious robe of deeds,
Be waiting for me up there.

TAKE ME TO A PLACE

Take me to a place Lord
Where I can rest in you
Place the serenity in my soul
As only you can do.
Place my spirit in that realm
Of joyous annointed bliss
Where you abide within my heart
And the feeling of love complete.
Place my mind on a platter
Of overwhelming peace
Where all you say, and every move you make
Will increase my measure of faith.
Take me Lord where my feet
Will be planted and stayed stedfast
Where I can always stay in place
And the past is left in the past.
Fold me under your wing so sweet
As to hide me from the storm
Lift me up as only you can
In your loving arms.
Take me to a place Lord
Where the quiet is heard so loud
For in you is this blessed place
And in you my soul will abide.

LIVING IN DARKNESS

Some of us are living in darkness
Walking with our eyes wide shut
Not knowing the thing that is needed
Is God, who loves us so much
We only see things as we want to
Afraid to take that leap of faith
Because the devil has closed our eyes
By telling us we can wait
My Father says come to me now
And give my love a try
I'll take the blindfold off
I'll open up your eyes
For if you'll trust and believe
In all I tell you to do
The darkness will fade away
And you can walk in the light of truth
I did not come here to harm you
Or put confussion in your head
I've come to release and save you
From the shadow of darkness instead
Stop looking for your freedom in delusions
Walking with your eyes wide shut
For I am the light in your darkness
And I've come to lift you up

FORGIVNESS

There is a pouch within our heart
Where forgivness is kept so safe.
That oozes out when needed
At the proper time and place.
Forgivness is not a thing
That's so hard to do
Just look at all the things
God has forgiven you.
It is also commanded ,
And not a heavy load
When you know it's very much needed
To save your heart and soul.
And don't let the devil tell you
Forgivness is not required
To enter into heaven
For once again he lied.
My God said He would forgive me
If only I repent and ask,
He made it all so easy
He made it a light-weight task.
So if you want to live right
And someday see His face,
Forgivness plays a large part
In your everyday walk with faith.
So release it everyday
To always remain in His will,
And you'll be surprised, maybe even amazed
At how easy it is to forgive!

LET IT GO — LET IT BE

*She heard her name being called out loud
By the angels singing a song
And in a voice so humble and sweet
She noticed a special tone.
With a depth of repentance and a love so deep
Her tears she began to shed
As she softly whispered, His name in praise
And slowly bowed her head.
Let it go and let it be
Are the words that filled the air
Coming from this most merciful song
To the heavy heart that was there.
She had no idea, of the meaning
Or from whence these words had come
So deeply planted within her soul
As none had been there before.
Let it go and let it be
Is all that she could hear,
As she fell to her knees, opened her mouth
And filled the room with prayer.
For there was no knowledge, that the burden she held
Was the theme in which they sang
And it was Jesus, telling her
To leave it in our Fathers hands..*

THE STORM

During your time of battle
With the things you fight the most
You'll learn to trust in Jesus
With all your heart and soul.
Jesus said come to me
With all your troubles and cares
For all the things, you bring to me
I went to the cross to bare.
All through your sleepless nights
And slow approaching dawns
I'll stand tall amist you
With loving and out stretched arms.
Oh, but let your souls rest
In the beauty of mine owm
During your day of struggle
I'll be with you during the storm.
And while you're patiently waiting
For your storm to pass
I'll stand with you, under every cloud
As I promise your storm won't last.
If you'll just open your heart
And know I'm by your side
For through your storm I'll carry you
And in my refuge, you can hide.
I'll speak to each of your problems
As they roll along
And hold your hand, as I keep you safe
Even after your storm has gone.

LOVE

Love is giving all of you,
Without expectation of pay.
An unexplainable desire to please,
While serving with a smile each day.
Love cannot be measured or conqured,
For it's way too smart for that,
Love just happens when you least expect it,
Without warning you in advance.
Love is the feeling of freedom,
From the depth of your heart so deep,
For the joy of someone elses blessings,
That was given by God himself.
You cannot grab it or tease it,
For it will win in the end,
You cannot hold it hostage,
For it knows your heart from within.
Love has no envy,
Nor anger or grief,
Just filled to capacity
Of goodwill and grace.
And love is a very fragile thing,
Like the fragility of the butterfly wing.
For it will make your heart complete,
If you cherish it to it's highest esteem.
It quenches the thirst of your hearts belief,
With an uncontrollable joy,
Like the water from the well of peace,
And an embrace from our Lord.
Love is the best, part of life,
And it's given to us for free,
For it is the most rewarding gift,
That can be given by you or me.

THE EARNED INSCRIPTION

I kept silent, silent as a lamb
Filled with words, I dare not speak
Slanderous voices I did hear
While a believing heart I did seek.
You placed a blindfold to cover my eyes
In hopes that I wouldn't see
The faces of the unjust ones
The ones that were taunting me.

And yet I still loved you

You laid a robe upon my back
While my blood did run slow
But no tainted blood could be found
Throughout my body flow.
For my blood did hold your future
As the scars were opened wide
And all your freedom did rest in me
From this body so worn and tired..

And yet I still loved you

You placed a hat of thorns
Upon my troubled head
Trying to make me confess
But silent I remained instead.
Not a sound or whimper did I make
To enhance the violent crowd
As a teardrop shed in silence
To never be seen out loud.

And yet I still loved you

For all the suffering had earned Him
An inscripted cross that read
THIS IS JESUS THE KING OF THE JEWS
Placed right above His head

And yet he still loves us

IN A VISION

Sometimes some things are placed, right before our eyes

I saw in a passing vision
A wayward blowing wind
Filled with unbelief and fear
Being caught by a fearless man
It seemed as if he stood
As tall as the mountains high
He had an army of many angels
Marching by his side.
His feet were made of solid stone
And with each step the earth did tremble
Slowly pacing himself along
To catch each wayward wind assembled
I reached out my hand to him
And he looked at me in awe
Then gently touched my fingertips
To let me know who he was
He opened his mouth to speak
And oh how the wind did blow
As a strong and powerful voice
Did rapidly overflow
I've come to let you know
I'll catch all of your wayward winds
For I am larger than all your fears
For I'm the one "I AM"

I tried to gaze beyond
To see all the things he'd caught
Instead I felt him cover me
As time just seem to stop.

A SILENT WHISPER

As I looked out, at the ones,
That nailed me to the cross,
I knew I had to help them,
I knew their souls were lost.
I knew then, it was not a choice,
But a very much needed must,
To show the world of a father,
Filled with joy, hope and trust.
You see, I know my father, He is a man
That's much more truer than true,
And the silent whisper, that I give
I give because of you!
I whisper and ask him Father,
Forgive them please for me.
For they are all lost souls,
And they know not what they do,
I ask him Father, show them mercy,
And lots and lots of grace,
And let the Holy Spirit
Return Lord in my place.
I know that I must go away,
But I'm never gone too far,
And I ask you Father, to let me
Forever remain in their hearts.
I ask Him Father, to keep them safe,
And let them never stray,
For I want to see them once again
On a much, much brighter day.
So remember this, one and all
And whatever you may do
Know this silent whisper I give
I give because of you!!!!

CHANGE THOSE CLOTHES

As Joshua stood, before the angel of God
And the one known for deceit,
The message that, was given to him
Was meant for you and me.
He was told, to take off those clothes
And take off the filth of sin,
For I have put rich garments on you
And I'm ready to bring you in.
You'll sit among the chosen ones
In whom you do believe,
No longer will you have to live
Among the ones who are deceived.
Take off those filthy garments
And live with peace within,
For I have washed you in the blood
And rid you of all your sins.
So this message is to reveal
A life that has yet to come,
A life filled with happiness
And angels on the run.
For all these filthy clothes you wear
Represent your sins and shame
And if you do not change them soon
Your burdens are sure to remain.
For I have put clean garments on you
And I'm ready to bring you in,
And watch those filthy clothes you wore
Turn to blessings, instead of sins.

BLOOD SHED

As God looked down from Heaven,
I can almost hear Him say,
I had to watch with a heavy heart,
As you hurt my son today!
I had to sit and watch you,
As you nailed Him to the cross,
All this done for the lack of trust,
But without it, all souls would be lost.
It's a day filled with darkness,
And gloom all around,
One that I must go through,
To make sure peace can be found.
You see that is my child,
And I do love Him so,
But He must leave your world today,
As we all watch Him go.
With tears in my eyes, I have watched
As you have made Him bleed,
This saviour who is a part of me,
So filled with the blood you need.
On this day I do declare,
An oath to you so true,
This will be the last time,
I'll let Him bleed for you.
For I have always loved you,
And I'll never leave you alone,
But it's time for my love to return
It's time for Him to come home.
On this day I have sacrificed
My only son for you,
Now let me see, what you'll sacrifice,
In the things you say and do.

HEIP ME LORD

Prayer changes things
And this I know is true
For you have answered so many for me
And I know it could only be you.
So as I drop to my knees
And lift my hands in praise
I'll slowly close them tightly together
And turn my praise to prayer.

Lord help me understand
The meaning of love more clear
To help the non-believers
Learn how to draw you near.
I ask that I might be able
To help someone today
To ease the feeling of lonliness
And help the pain to fade.
Help me choose the words
To dry up some ones tears
And fill their hearts with joy
To replace the sorrow there.
Let me help someone
Exchange the fear with hope
And come to you, with a humble heart
To open that door that's closed.
Help me, help someone's mind
Rest in all your peace
So that all the worldly thoughts
Might quickly go with ease.
You see Lord, it's me again
Asking for a helping hand
To help me , help someone
To make it to the promise land.

COVER THESE BONES

When God sat down to write your life,
He knew how it would end.
He had the plans all set up,
From the time He did begin.
He already knew you inside out
From the top of your head to your feet,
For He had placed all things in you
So His requirements you would meet.
He took the frames of bones you see
And he covered them all with flesh,
He added his most Holy blood
And a spirit and soul came next.
He knew he had to add enough faith
To take you through the years,
He knew to add courage and hope
To help you face up to your fears.
Then He spoke to his Holy work
"I know that I'm not through,
for I must add the love of myself
to ensure I'm done with you.
for when I look at what I've made
from the frame of bones today,
I surrounded them with all that's needed
now I can most boldly say,
to all the creatures of heaven and earth
as you bow at the sound of my name,
the ones that I have just created,
will be the most sacred, in all of my domain.".

A WORD FROM YOU

Sometimes my heart will fill with joy,
From the thought of hearing the voice,
That will soothe the very anticipation,
On some things that I've prayed for.
For the urgency of my wanting things,
Will make me feel impatient,
But then I'll hear you speak,
With words of expectation.
You'll tell me to remember,
That you hold the key to my fate,
And never step ahead of you,
But behind you I should stay,
You'll tell me never to rush,
Into anything at all,
But always wait on you,
And you will answer my call.
You'll tell me not to run,
From the problem that is on hand,
But if I really have to run,
To run to you instead.
You'll tell me never give up,
On the dreams you've placed in me,
You'll tell me not to forget,
That my future, you have made.
You'll tell me being myself,
Is not all that I can be,
But all I can be is myself,
For you only made one of me.

HEAVEN BOUND

When we all get to heaven,
What a wonderful day it will be,
When once again we'll get to see,
Our friends and family.
The angels will greet us at the door,
With a smile upon their faces,
Showing us all around up there,
And showing the most holiest of places.
We'll greet each other with hugs and kisses,
And arms all linked together,
For we have traveled a mighty long way,
For this meeting going on in heaven.
With our hands all lifted in the air,
We'll sing our songs of praises,
Some singing, some dancing, some crying, some praying,
All done with joy and amazement.
We'll stroll the streets all paved with gold,
And never look back again,
For we have come to this great city,
And our new life has just began.
No darkness shall enter into this place,
Only light from eternity through,
This place called heaven, prepared long ago,
Prepared for me and you.
Oh, but that's not, the end of it yet,
The most important has yet to be mentioned,
The one we really long to see,
Is the face of our redeemer,
He'll smile with love and open arms
And greet us with a cheer,
And look to His father, our Lord, our God,
And say thank you for letting them enter!!

MY INHERITANCE

Jesus I thank you every day,
For going to that cross for me,
And I shall never forget the way
Of how you set me free.
You made sure, that I could live,
In a world of peace,
You left me with a treasure box,
With my in-heri-tance.
I opened up this treasure box,
And my heart did overflow,
When I did see, all you'd left for me,
To help me overcome.
You left me with lots of hope,
To get me through the day,
You left me with many options.
To help me choose the way.
You left me with Grace and favor,
And oh what a pair they make,
Together they help me plunge ahead,
And to keep my footsteps straight.
You left me with days of peace,
And nights that are filled with joy,
You left me with the Holy Spirit,
And a praise down deep in my heart.
You turned my darkness into light,
And gave me new eyes to see,
You offered me a new way of living,
In this treasure box for me.
This treasure box, is a book,
Called the Bible you see,
With all the golden wisdom you'll need
To claim your in-heri-tance.

OH PRECIOUSLY, SILENT ROBE

What happened to you, oh silent robe,
That covered my Saviours back?
The one that was placed to embarrass Him,
While hiding those awful whelps.
Where did you come from, where were you stored,
For no one will ever know.
Were you placed there for that one reason,
To put on a one man show?
Did they rip you up, and tear you to shreds,
Once the damage was done?
Did they really try hard to get rid of you,
After hiding my Saviours wounds?
Many unjust words were spoken that day,
But a most precious gift you foretook,
For you caught the innocent blood of Jesus,
And held it, as no man could.
You were there with each slap of the face,
And the thorns that were placed on His head,
You heard all the insults that were made,
You heard everything that was said.
You were there to see the horrible rage,
That was seen in every ones eyes,
With the hustling and bustling of stomping feet,
And angry words and cries.
You felt His most powerful blood,
As it soaked you through and through,
Oh precious and most silent robe,
I wonder what happened to you!!

THE BAPTISM

During some thought, I placed myself
On the bank of the river one day
Where John was busy baptizing
lost souls that were passing that way.
I watched them enter one by one
And I began to think
On what a blessing it really is
To be forgiven in a blink.
Next, my eyes started to wonder
At the sight of this one man
That stood there with a shimmer of glory
Surrounding both his hands.
I then drifted further in thought
And I could hear Him speak
As He looked toward John and so eagerly said
I'd like to be in the mix.
I'd like for you to baptize me
In the same way as the others
In the presence of all these men
And in the presence of my Father.
And as I saw, Him go under
I could see the ripples a rolling
As the son of God did soon come up
And a dove then land on His shoulder.
I could see the rays of light
Shining ever, ever so bright
surrounding His Holy body
and His robe made of white.
It seemed as if He looked at me
with a gentle smile of delight
as He turned and walked away
in His glorious power and might.

THOU PREPARAST A TABLE

During a night of uninterrupted converversation with you,
I heard you speak of a table, being prepared just for me !

Grace and Mercy were seated there,
To ensure me a well blessed meal,
They bowed their heads and opened their mouths,
As they offered up this prayer.
Lord we pray you keep her,
Under your arm so strong
And bless this table before her
Prepared for her alone.
You placed before me riches,
I never thought of before,
On that day you blessed me,
With that prepared table of love,
You prepared a table before me,
That was filled with so much joy,
In the presence of mine enemies,
Where the hurt would be no more.
You had made, all my trials,
A delightful thing of the past,
For you had already told me,
Trouble won't always last.
You prepared a table before me,
With hope and peace combined,
They fell atop, of a white linen sheet,
As the problems were left behind,
And all the wrongs done me,
Fell at my enemies feet,
For they were placed under the table,
The table prepared for me.
And as my enemies sat there,
They had to watch me eat,
The bounty from this tabel,
So beautifully arrayed for me!!

UNDER HIS CLOAK OF POWER

There's miracles not seen
And dreams not dreamed
There's blessings to claim
And all kinds of things

There's peace of mind
And rest devine
There's joy filled days
There's forgiveness and praise

There's strength and light
And star filled nights
There's mercy and grace
There's hope and faith

There's love and truth
Salvation strong
There's calm and peace
All troubles gone

And you're freed from yokes
With a silent approach
There's a new life to live
And much more to give

There's caring and shareing
And lots of praying
There's repentence of sin
So come on in.............................UNDER HIS CLOAK OF POWER

UNCHAINED SEED OF FAITH

I have a space within my heart
Where my Savior comes to rest
I can feel the footsteps of His spirit
Treading lightly, as He paces himself
I can feel the healing seething
Through each bitter hold of pain
I can feel the passion of His love
With each breath of air substained
I can feel Him rest upon my burdens
As they attempt to hide
I can feel Him release His power
To unchain the faith inside
I can feel Him breathe with every beat
That my heart doth make
I can feel the joy of His spirit
As He takes another step
For He catches every stone
That's being thrown at me you see
As He looks my troubles in the eyes
To prevent them from looking at me
Upon my heart His spirit rest
With His annointed and glorious steps
Pacing Himself so gently
To ensure my needs are met
And He has placed His hand of hope
Upon my very soul
And through my heart His blood does flow
To keep me forever more
And now I know He's here
Within my heart to stay
And He has made that mustard seed
Become an unchained seed of faith

COVERED SMILE

A teardrop rolled from my eyes last night
As I began to think.
On all the goodness in this world
And how soon it may be extinct.
My heart was in this special place
And this I cannot deny
It was turning itself inside out
As that tear had become a cry.
So many things have come my way
Some I don't understand
And yet you uphold, my very soul
With the righteousness of your hand.
I know I have no right to complain
About anything at all
For you have always been here
And you've never ignored my call.
You're not the one that placed the wetness
In these eyes so pure
Or placed a frown, upon this face
With a covered smile of tears.
For you have been, and always done
So much in my life it's true
So less complaining, and more understanding
You'll hear from my mouth to you.
Now you have filled ,my life with joy
There's no room for denial or dispute
And thus this covered smile of tears
Has become a smile of truth!

FROM YOUR FATHER

I walked along beside you
And you knew not that I was there,
But it was I, that ever so softly
Place the wind that blew your hair.
I gently took a hold of your hand,
As you began to stall,
I did not want you to stumble,
I did not want you to fall.
I took you step by step,
From the time you had begun,
To ensure that you would live Holy,
In the many years to come.
I watched you as you stop to eat,
And blessed the food, head bowed,
You called my name so earnestly,
And that's when I heard you vow,
You said that you would keep me
In your thoughts both day and night,
And that I would always be
In your heart, mind and sight.
For this I say thank you
With a blessing all so true.
To know that you are thinking of me,
While I'm also thinking of you.

Your Heavenly Father.

HELP

I asked my angel to speak to you
Cause I knew not what to say,
My words seem to evade my thoughts
In such an unusual way.
There are some things I need to speak,
And I feel a word or two short,
To express my feelings, about these things,
That are coming from my heart.
I want not, to step outside the box
With words unbecoming to you,
So I asked for help, from my angel of truth
To get my message through.
I ask for strength to lead the way,
For the things I cannot solve,
I need your favor in my life,
To help me get along.
So I ask you Father to hear my plea,
As I pray so true,
For these feelings, that I feel,
To bring me closer to you,
I do not want, to take much time
Cause I know you're busy to,
I just need a little help and strength today,
The kind that comes only from you.

HOW DO I SAY THANKS?

How do I say thanks,
For all you've done for me?
You've lifted me up, when I was down,
You've given me the victory.
You've opened my heart, and placed your love,
Upon my every need,
So tell me how, somebody please,
How do I say thanks?
I cannot buy you anything
That you can put on display,
I cannot send you flowers,
Try as much as I may.
I cannot send you a greeting card,
To help you along your way,
So tell me how, somebody please,
How do I say thanks?
I cannot pick you up,
To take you out to dine,
You attended the most esquisite feast,
Ever seen by mankind.
I cannot come to visit,
For if I could, I would,
And maybe say a few things,
That maybe I know I should.
I know you need no earthly things,
Because the earth belongs to you,
So in my attempt to say thank you Lord,
I hope "I LOVE YOU" will do.

LAST NIGHT'S BREEZE

We've heard, we've read, we've talked about, your overwhelming love,
and how we can place it, in our hearts, to become forever stored.....

I heard you call my name last night,
Through the calm and gentle wind,
As it so softly blew it's breath,
And captured my heart from within.
It calmed all the uprooted moods,
That the world had earlier placed,
Into my very being of self,
As it quietly brushed my face.
I watched the dark and beautiful sky,
As it filled itself with stars,
I said a soft and humble prayer,
As you listened from afar.
I turned my face into the breeze,
To take in all I could,
That's when I felt more close to you,
From that slow blowing breeze of love.

THAT SONG

As I was driving around today,
I heard a familiar song,
It touched my heart in such a way,
I started to hum along.
It made me go back to a time,
A time when I was young,
When you were told to always listen,
And always mind your tongue.
Then my spirit started to stir,
As I thought upon the words,
It seemed as if it was meant for me,
That song that I just heard.
It made me start to wander,
About a thing or two,
But most of all, it reminded me,
Of the miraculous things you do.
It was as if you were seated there,
Beside me holding my hand,
And I could almost hear you say,
I AM WHO I SAY I AM !
I am everything you need,
In this life and the next,
I have your entire life and future,
Already made out and planned.
So let my spirit fill you,
And continue to embrace your heart,
And let that song, that you heard,
Be a blessing that never stops.

MY SOUL BELONGS TO YOU

Just the knowledge of knowing, that I've been touched
by your hand...........
even before I was in my mother's womb, and I have breathe your breath, as you so lovingly gave....
and had a smell of your aura, even before my birth,........................
My soul belongs to you....
For there is no darkness, your eyes can't peel,
and beyond all truth you know
and there's no wrong in your word,
My soul belongs to you....
I could live 2,000 years, and never know your thoughts.......
and yet , you need only a glimps.....and all my secrets become known....to you and you alone...as my spirit quivers at the sound
of your name..........
My soul belongs to you....

UNDER HIS WINGS

As the sand is blown across the desert floor,
and the waves wash along the sea,
so safe and cozy it will be,
under his wings of love.

As a gentle breeze, cross your face,
and a simple thought enters your mind,
the calmness will carry you to a spirit so sweet,
under his wings of love.

A wonderful feeling will fill your heart,
as you rest in His peace divine,
no problems, no pain, no tears, just gain,
under his wings of love.

Your soul will soar, as the eagle in flight,
and will not get weiry or faint,
just a glorious bliss, with joy admist,
under his wings of love.

IMAGINE

As I closed my eyes, I thought I did see,
Two of God's angels escorting me,
One on the left and one on the right,
As they were taking me, to the throne one night.
They had their wings, spread all wide, as they spoke to me,
Saying, we have something here to show you,
Something you've been longing to see.
I stood to take one small step, then slowly made it two,
As they each held me by an arm, to gently guide me through.
I could feel the warmth of your great love, in each step that we took,
I had to stop..... and just stand still, being amazed as I took a look.
As the throne of God then drew near, the angels sang so sweet,
Singing it's so good to see you, your prayers have brought you here.
As my knees started to tremble, and my head did slowly bow,
I said a prayer so softly, as they began to sing out loud,
Lord thank you for blessing her, and keeping her all so safe,
And most of all thank you Lord, for letting her see this place.
My drifting mind, then let me hear, the words I love you my child,
But here you can't remain, cause you're just visiting for a while,
And when I see you bow your head and see you bending your knees,
It's all so pleasing, yes very pleasing ,very pleasing to me.
So the next time you close your eyes to say a prayer so clear,
Remember I'll be watching you, and waiting to bring you here.
For it's a beautiful place to visit, but it's not time to stay,
It's just a glimps of your new home, that you will see someday.
And it was all, so very real, or so it really seemed
But then the angels did wake me, to tell me it was only a dream!

JESUS OF NAZARETH

Hey Jesus of Nazareth...Where are you going with that cross on your back?

"I'm going to a place where you can't go,
to remove your sins, because I love you so."

But Jesus of Nazareth..Why do you carry that old rugged cross?

"I carry this cross to it's resting place, I carry it because I care.
I carry it because it's a need for you, and it's one less cross for you to bare."

Well Jesus of Nazareth..What can I do, to help lighten your heavy load?

"You must not remove a thing, to make the load less heavy,
all things must remain as they are, for your lives to become less bitter.
You do not want to remove a thing, for that is my purpose of being,
it's for your sake that I carry this cross, to remove your transgressions and sins"

Oh, but Jesus of Nazareth..Why do you look so tired?

"Tired? I wear these thorns upon my head,
to help your dreams and thoughts,
and the stripes I wear upon my back,
is for the healing of your body and soul.
I wear the blood and bruises,
from the beating I took from you,
I wear the sweat and pain,
so you'll know I am the way and the truth,
For I might look tired, on the outside you see,
but that's for the eye of the beholder,
cause the light that shines on the inside of me,
was placed here by my Father.
And through it all, I must confess,
my love for you remains,
for I, just like my Father's word,
will never, ever change" !!!

AS I SLEPT

You took a chair, and sat by my bed
And decided to stay all night.
You held my hand, as I slept
Til the early morning sunrise.
You appointed angels to stand at my feet
And some were at my head,
All during the night, they did stay
As I slept upon my bed.
But you my Lord sat by my side,
And never did you leave.
You took me through the long, long night,
While upon my bed I did sleep.
You let my mind rest with peace
So no evil thing could creep,
No displaced dreams or misplaced things
Did occur as I did sleep.
For I know my life is in your hands
To do with as you please,
But just the knowing of your presence there
Did keep my soul at ease.
So I thank you Lord for watching me
As my eyes were tightly closed,
I knew that I was in safe hands,
As the night would slowly unfold.
And I thank you Lord for being here,
To be the first to whom I'd speak
As you gently whispered and called my name,
To awaken me from my sleep...

THOUGHTS

THOUGHTS 1

1. Your past is exactly that....leave it there !....HE DID!!

2. Your attitude can take you far, or leave you far behind !!

3. Why say luck? Things happen by Faith and belief !!

4. To ignore someone's hardships....
   could be the loss of a very good friendship !!

5. Hope's not lost...you just have to know where to find it !!

6. Your reputation preceeds you.....
   make sure it's worthy to follow !!!

7. Blessings are showing up everywhere.....
    not only in recieviing....theres also giving !!!!

8. everyday belongs to the Lord.......
   but on Sunday it's CAPITALIZED !!!!!!!

THOUGHTS 2

1. If you'll strengthen your spirit, you'll weaken the flesh!!
      PRAISE HIS HOLY NAME

2. If you can't--out think Him
   or----------out speak Him
   neither------out box Him
THEN WHY WOULD YOU THINK YOU CAN----OUT RUN HIM

3. We're on the hi-way to Heaven---Why would you take an exit?

4. A friendship built on trust, is bound to last,
   A friendship built on lust, is assured to pass.

5. Fear is like a virus, once released, it can affect many!

THOUGHTS 3

1. There's one thing in life. that will always be true,
   that in this life, you can only be you.

2. Unlike a rubber band, the truth was not meant to be stretched.

3. On the other side of darkness, there's a light to be found.

4. Gossipers walk on thin ice.......whoops.......watch your step.

5. Some egos don't have to be fed......they feed on themselves.

6. You are....because He said....I AM

7. Don't let your words preceed your thoughts.

THOUGHTS 4

1. God hears, God does, God knows.

2. Not knowing is the problem, learning is the solution.

3. There's no room for curiosity in another ones business.

4. Easiest recipi to a good conversation is listening with care, and speaking with caution.

5. Let that one of a kind be you.

6. A quiet temper and easy spirit will help control a loud mouth and a quick hand.

7. Holding things in can be harmful to your health, it closes the thought valves.

8. Exercising your body is good for your health, exercising your faith is good for your soul.

9. Don't indulge yourself in other people's conflicts, unless you plan to make them your own.

10. Trying to be someone else, is denying yourself the privilege of being you.

THOUGHTS 5

1. If you really want your secrets kept....keep them yoursef.

2. There's no expiration date on faith.

3. I have yet to see a problem solve itself.

4. Trying to be someone else, is denying yourself the priviledge of being you.

5. Look, listen and learn a lot

6. Character building does not come with a blue print.

7. Never say can't....can't will get you nothing.....
   and make you have even less.

8. While you're running from God... He's slow walkning you down.

9. You can't box with God. He has a mean right hook of righteousness and a hard left jab to back it up.

10. WONDER WHAT THEY'RE DOING UP IN HEAVEN TODAY...

11. Because ones' eyes ..are closed to some things....
    does not mean .... they do not see.

THOUGHTS 6

1. God is not here for a short term relationship, He's in it for the long haul.

2. If you start your day off with prayer, you'll end it with lots of grace.

3. The best way to hear Him speak, is for you to stop talking.

4. Put your order in today, salvation is free.

5. You should stand tall as the cedar, and mighty as the oak, unstoppable, unchangeable, unmoveable.

6. Making little of a problem, does not make it go away....handle it !

7. Let the Holy rivers of water flow through your body, to make streams for others to see.

8. Living God's way is easy...

9. For every one step you take, God will take two, now just imagine what will happen if you run.

10. Let God not only dwell in your heart, let Him dwell deep down in your soul also.

THOUGHTS 7

1. "I AM" is already here...Hallelujah give Him praise

2. Judging others, will get you the judgement of your life.

3. Let your robe of deeds, be tightly knit and well sewn together

4. There's no extented warrenty on life...Stay prayed up

5. He's not sleeping...just waiting for you to wake up

6. Even in His shadow....there's light

7. Turn your thoughts into reality....think BIG

8. When you open a door to the past, sometimes it's best to close it quickly

9. Love has no gender, race, creed or color..and it comes in all sizes

10. Smile

11. He did not owe his life for us...but we owe him our life for his.

12. If you'll walk with Jesus..there's a gaurentee that you'll never get lost

13. Put your imagination away....one day we'll see Him face to face.

14. Give your heart to its rightful owner....God

15. Remember....He didn't have to do it....but He did..

THOUGHTS 8

1. Be ye also ready..... for I will not announce my arrival

2. Let us live each day to the fullest... but...have a yearning desire for a better tomorrow

3. He knew your secret before you told Him.... He's all knowing

4. Life's too short to sit and whine about the things we could've had
   We need to be thankful everyday for the things we already have

5. Seize every opporunity to give Him praise

6. If you lose your soul here on earth.... what will you take to heaven ?

7. You cannot get desirable results with undesirable actions

8. Don't count yourself out..if He fed 5,000..He'll feed you too

9. What the world needs now is more love..more caring..more helping more sharing...less malice..less crulty..less hate

10. There is no night in heaven.....and everyday is glorious

11. Don't quote things others say....know them for yourself....read and learn

12. Disabilities does not mean inabilities....

13. With an unwaivering heart to love and a spirit to understand....
    we can't help but live with hope

14. Stir it up..pour it up..pick it up..we're talking about faith..preach pastor   preach !!!

15. When you cannot find the words....let your angels moan

THOUGHTS 9

1. God is perfect, and has it all.....we are imperfect and want it.

2. You cannot change someone else....without some change yourself

3. Thank you for another chance to say.... "Thank you for another day"

4. He didn't give us life to destroy....He gave us life to enjoy.

5. We know the mind is a terrible thing to waste...but what about the soul?

6. If you want to wear your robe of white...stop playing in the dirt.

7. God's word is his bond....unbreakable ..unmovable..unstoppable.

8. Ooops there He goes again....He just keeps on blessing me...

9. If you want to stay in the will of God....get into the will of His son..

10. And let us pray....and praise His name....

11. Never jump to a conclusion, or assume an assumption,
    just admit that you don't know

12. Leave the things of the past where they should be,
    for you need room for the future to grow

13. In the mind you conceive it, in the heart you believe it,
    by your faith you recieve it.

14. Your imagination will get things started, your faith will make them go.

THOUGHTS FOR NOW

1. The complications in your life, should never rise above the paise from your heart

2. How can you expect more, when you give absolutly nothing

3. Love is giving all of you, without expectation of pay

4. Some collect stamps, some collect coins, but God is a soul collector

5. How bad can your life be? Did you hear about Christ dying on the cross?

6. If I lose my reasoning, then I lose my way .If I give up on me, then what more can I expect of others

7. Our Father said come as you are...not stay as you were

8. I'll stand my ground and not be defeated, and giving up is not an option

9. Just like you, I was only passing through

10.. Faith is the key to your fate

11. For every praise sent up, a prayer is answered

12. Always put God first and see how great second can be

DEDICATION

I dedicate this book to you my Father. May the words you've given me bring honor and glory to your Holy name. Thank you for loving me, And for this I give you praise.

I have been blessed with two of the greatest children ever, and I thank God for them both, I often remark that my Father could've given them to someone else, but He decided to place them in my care. I deeply love them both. They are very special, and have grown into wonderful adults, who have given me terrific grandchildren..Roger, Ariana, and Aliyah. Donna and Kelvin, you make me proud to even know you, thank you for being who you are. You two have always given me reasons to be the proudest mom on earth, now I will try to make you proud of me.

Love Mom

CPSIA information can be obtained
at www.ICGtesting.com
Printed in the USA
FFOW05n1242191016